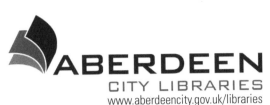

...hters

Clare Oliver

Photographs: Chris Fairclough

VV
FRANKLIN WATTS
LONDON•SYDNEY

First published in 2002 by
Franklin Watts
96 Leonard Street
London
EC2A 4XD

Franklin Watts Australia
45–51 Huntley Street
Alexandria
NSW 2015

© Franklin Watts 2002

A CIP catalogue record for this book is available
from the British Library.

ISBN 0 7496 4669 1
Dewey Decimal Classification Number 363.3

Series Editor: Jackie Hamley
Cover Design: Peter Scoulding
Design: Sally Boothroyd

Photos
All commissioned photographs by Chris Fairclough.
The publishers would like to thank the following
for permission to use photographs:
www.shoutpictures.com
8, 9, 11, 12 (operator), 15, 27
Simon Russell 25 (display)
Phil Roach/ Rex Features 26

The author and publisher would especially like to thank White Watch at
Loughton Fire Station, Essex for giving their help and time so generously.

Printed in Malaysia

Contents

Meet the team

Night and day, firefighters are helping people all over the country.

At most fire stations, firefighters work in **shifts** – during the day or night – so there is always a full team on duty. Each team is called a **watch** and is named after a colour – white, blue, red or green.

helmet

mask

breathing equipment

torch

firefighting uniform

Firefighters wear special clothes to protect them when they are doing their job.

In this book, you will meet White Watch, firefighters from Loughton Fire Station in Essex.

Here's White Watch with their station commander, Vernon.

1 Darren **2** Ian **3** Brad **4** Steve **5** Bernie
6 Pete **7** Jamie **8** Alan **9** Vernon

Fighting fires

▦ **The main way firefighters help us is by rescuing people trapped in fires and by putting out fires.**

Firefighting is very dangerous work. Fires can start anywhere – in homes, schools or other buildings.

Thousands of litres of water will **extinguish** the flames in this hotel fire.

Firefighters extinguished the fire on this plane using foam. They used foam because water can make some kinds of fire worse.

Fires can happen when vehicles blow up, or when forests and fields catch fire.

Most fires happen by accident but some are started on purpose. This is called **arson**.

FACT

▷ In 1999, UK firefighters went to 935,500 **call-outs**. About 100,000 of these were arson.

▷ In January 2002, firefighters in Australia fought huge **bush fires** around Sydney. Many of these fires had been started by arsonists.

⊞ Firefighters' skills and equipment are useful in other emergencies, too.

Firefighters' powerful cutters can free people after car, train or plane crashes. The pumps they carry can remove water from flooded buildings. And their hoses can help wash away chemical spills.

Firefighters wear special **chemical protection suits** to keep them safe when they work with chemicals.

Before they take them off, firefighters clean their chemical protection suits in a special shower.

Firefighters use their ladders to climb up and check that buildings are safe after a storm, fire or other problem. They can also use their ladders to rescue people from floods. Sometimes they even rescue pets!

Firefighters use their ladders to check the safety of this factory after a fire.

A woman is rescued from the first floor of her house. She was trapped by floodwater for two days.

" I remember rescuing a very wriggly, frightened little kitten. You should have seen the face of the girl who owned it. What a picture! "
Darren, leading firefighter

Sound the alarm!

When there is a fire, someone has to call the Fire Service.

The call is put through to an operator at one of the Fire Service's control centres. The operator asks the caller questions about the fire, and sends a call slip, like a fax message, to the fire station nearest the fire.

The call slip tells the firefighters where to go and which fire engine to use.

The operator contacts the fire station nearest to the emergency.

Everyone's firefighting uniform is hanging up, ready for a call-out.

▶ *Firefighters call their fire engines* **appliances**.

▶ *Loughton has two different appliances, a* **water tender** *and a* **rescue pump**.

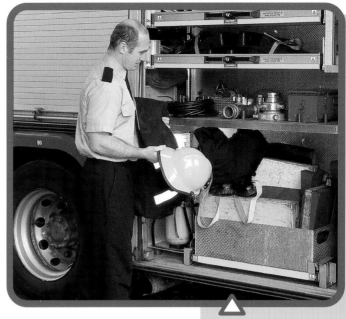

When the **duty officer** at the fire station receives the call slip, he or she sounds the alarm and lets everyone know which engine will be sent.

Today, Brad will drive the rescue pump. He stows his uniform in the side.

Off to the fire – sirens blare and lights flash!

■■ When firefighters arrive at the fire, they take the equipment they need off the fire engine.

The water tender engine arrives first. The driver, Steve, connects a hose to the water supply by opening a water **hydrant**.

Driver Steve fixes the hose to the hydrant.

breathing equipment

Firefighter Darren puts on his breathing equipment. This allows him to breathe in the smoky building.

air cylinder

The air is stored in a **cylinder** worn on the back.

Firefighters rescue a child from a house fire.

The firefighters go into the building. They stick close together, hosing the flames and searching for anyone trapped inside. They help people out of the building as quickly as possible.

Our uniforms are heat-resistant and our helmets protect our heads. But going into a burning building is very dangerous. We keep in touch with each other by radio.

Brad, firefighter

Around the fire

Firefighters have to be careful to use just enough water to put out a fire.

If firefighters use too much water, they might flood the building. Firefighters may also use foam to fight some fires. They make sure no foam goes down the drains as this could affect the water supply.

Covering the drains with sand bags keeps foam out of the water supply.

FACT

▷ *Carelessness with cigarettes and matches causes most house fires.*

▷ *Other causes of house fires include burning chip pans, faulty electrics, and open fires left without fireguards.*

Firefighter Jamie asks a neighbour what she saw.

Sub-officer Alan will have to write a report later, so the firefighters ask questions about how the fire started. They also look for clues inside the building.

When the fire is out, the firefighters clean the street using their hoses.

Cleaning the street after a fire gets rid of all the ash and debris.

Fire drill

White Watch spend their time between call-outs on training exercises, or drills.

Firefighters never know when the next emergency will happen. To make sure they are prepared, they practise working together and using all the equipment.

Sub-officer Alan is responsible for training the other firefighters.

This engine has a very long ladder. It is called an **aerial ladder platform** and it helps firefighters reach people trapped high up.

SIMON ALP340

Firefighters learn to use the aerial ladder platform.

The station yard has a tall practice tower which is used for ladder rescue **drills**. The sub-officer gives tips so the team will be able to save time in a real emergency.

Once you've had a night-time call-out, you realise why drills are important. You know exactly where everything is and just how to use it – even in the dark!
Pete, firefighter

Firefighters lower a **dummy** from the practice tower.

At the ready!

At the beginning of each shift, the firefighters check each of the engines and make sure that no equipment is missing.

Ian and Bernie check that all the equipment is on board.

The firefighters order anything they need. Trevor from head office delivers replacements to all of the 51 fire stations in Essex.

Keeping the tank full of diesel means the engine is always ready to go.

> " *After a call-out we clean the appliance and fill up the tank with diesel. We don't go to a garage, though – there's a pump in the station yard.* "
>
> **Ian, firefighter**

Fire engines carry lots of equipment.

1 portable pump, used to pump water from flooded buildings **2** chemical protection suit **3** resuscitator, used to start someone breathing again **4** suction hose, used to get extra water from lakes or rivers **5** breathing equipment **6** environmental spill kit, used to mop up chemical spills, for example

The firefighters check the equipment again after every call-out. Something might have been left behind or the air in the cylinders may have been used up.

Trevor drops off full air cylinders and takes away the empty ones.

Crash rescue

Many of White Watch's call-outs are to car accidents.

Two large motorways run through the area served by Loughton Fire Station. Firefighters wear bright yellow coats at crash scenes so that other drivers can see them.

At traffic accidents, firefighters work closely with police and ambulance crews.

> *Everyone works together at traffic accidents – the important thing for all of us is to save lives.*
> **Jamie, firefighter**

After a crash, vehicles sometimes burst into flames. The firefighters then have to extinguish the fire.

They also use their powerful cutting equipment to work through twisted metal and free any people trapped inside the vehicles.

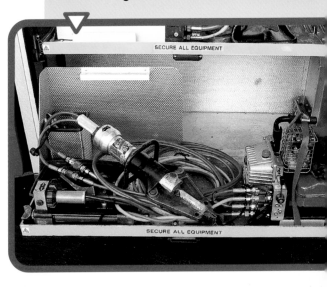

The rescue pump carries special equipment that can cut through metal.

Firefighters use their cutting equipment to free a trapped driver.

Firefighters work hard to make sure that fires never happen.

Firefighters visit schools and hold open days at the fire station to teach people about fire safety.

Firefighters take their engine along to schools so that children can see the equipment on board.

> *The earlier children learn about how to prevent fires, the better. What's really good is when you see the same children a year later and they've remembered your message.*
>
> **Bernie, leading firefighter**

Pete advises the head teacher about fire safety in the school.

Fire extinguishers need to be tested to check they still work properly.

Firefighters also inspect public buildings such as schools, offices, hotels and restaurants. They make sure that all the fire extinguishers are working and that there are enough clear fire exits.

This display at the fire station shows people how quickly fires can start in the kitchen.

Help in action

⚅ Around the world, firefighters are saving other people's lives and risking their own.

Firefighters rescue people from fires, and also from earthquakes, volcanoes, avalanches and floods. They find victims of mining accidents, air crashes, bomb explosions – and other totally unexpected disasters.

In 2001, New York's firefighters showed great bravery after the World Trade Center was attacked. More than 340 firefighters lost their lives.

Firefighters rescue people trapped in cars and buildings after this earthquake in the United States.

Bush fires like this one in Australia happen in hot, dry weather.

Sometimes, it is possible to predict the sorts of disasters firefighters will face. In Australia and the United States, for example, firefighters face raging bush fires and forest fires nearly every year. These may burn out of control for weeks or even months, destroying crops and homes and endangering lives.

Everybody helps the firefighters at these times. People help them by putting out the smaller fires in and around houses, leaving the firefighters free to extinguish the large fires in the bush or forest.

Further information

It takes four years to become a fully-trained firefighter. This begins with 20 weeks at a training centre. After that, the firefighter starts at a fire station to continue training.

To find out more about the Fire Service you could visit:

www.fire.org.uk/kids/home.htm
www.fireservice.co.uk/children.htm

Or read:

A Day in the Life of a Firefighter

by Carol Watson
Franklin Watts, 1995

To find out more about the Fire Service in Australia, visit: www.fpaa.com.au

Index

A ROSE FOR
PINKERTON

Story and pictures by
STEVEN KELLOGG

FREDERICK WARNE

That lovable but untrainable Great Dane, Pinkerton,
seems lonely. He needs a friend, and a sweet, cuddly kitten
like Rose should fill the bill perfectly. But Rose has ideas of
her own. *She* wants to be a Great Dane and she's scaring
poor Pinkerton out of his wits. As for Pinkerton—
he's crawling into the cat basket, eating cat food, and curling
up on people's laps. So it's off to the International Pet
Show to seek some expert advice. What results is one of
Steven Kellogg's zaniest, funniest romps ever.

Readers who cheered on Pinkerton in *Pinkerton, Behave!*
will applaud his return in Steven Kellogg's newest delight.

A Junior Literary Guild Selection in the U.S.A.

Published by Frederick Warne (Publishers) Ltd, London, 1982

ISBN 0 7232 2901 5

The process art consists of black line-drawings,
black halftones, and full-color washes. The black line
is prepared and photographed separately for greater
contrast and sharpness. The full-color washes and
the black halftones are prepared with ink, crayons,
and paints on the reverse side of the black line-drawing.
They are then camera-separated and reproduced as
red, blue, yellow, and black halftones.

And another for Helen

Sarah X

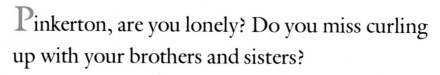

Pinkerton, are you lonely? Do you miss curling up with your brothers and sisters?

We should get some other Great Dane puppies to play with Pinkerton.

I think he's trying to tell you that he agrees with me.

One Great Dane is enough! The only other pet I would consider would be something small and quiet...like a goldfish.

I'll go find a friend for you, Pinkerton.

This is the perfect place!

Pinkerton couldn't curl up with a goldfish.

And he couldn't play with a bird.

Maybe a kitten would be just right!

It says here in my book that Great Dane puppies
and kittens can become good friends.

Here's a surprise for you and Pinkerton.
Her name is Rose.

It says in this book by Sarah Chattercat that Great
Dane puppies and kittens can become good friends.

He seems to like her.

Rose took over Pinkerton's sun spot.

She's eating his dinner.

I think Rose wants to be a Great Dane.

Oh, no!

Now Pinkerton is trying to be a kitten!

Let's go back to that pet show! I have a
few questions for Sarah Chattercat!

Rose! Come back!

Pinkerton will be safe with the kittens.
Help me find Rose.

Rose! Where are you?

I see her! She's in line for the Grand March of the Poodles!

I'd like to welcome our television audience to this stunning event and to introduce Dr. Aleasha Kibble of Canine University, who will present the Golden Poodle Trophy.

Stop the ceremony! Call the police! The Grand March
has been infiltrated by a feline impostor!

Excuse us, but that's our cat, Rose. She used to think she was a Great Dane but she's decided to be a poodle.

Ladies and gentlemen, the crowd and the poodles have gone berserk!

They are chasing the intruding cat towards the Castle of the Kittens!

There's a monster in the Castle of the Kittens.

Arrest that brute! He terrified our poodles, and they've all fainted!

Nonsense! This wonderful dog saved the kittens.
He's a hero!

Look! It's Rose!

Does she still think she's a poodle?
Or is she a Great Dane again?

She's purring!